JONATHAN ADLER

on HAPPY CHIC

➤ *Colors*

STERLING INNOVATION
An imprint of Sterling Publishing Co., Inc.

New York / London
www.sterlingpublishing.com

ACKNOWLEDGMENTS

I am the luckiest potter/decorator/retailer/author in the world because I get to collaborate with the most creative, brilliant, and hilarious people. Thank you to...

➵ **Photographers:** Jessica Antola, Colleen Duffley, Evan Joseph, Joshua McHugh, Ngoc Minh Ngo, Thomas Olcott, Albert Sanchez, Todd Selby, Jonathan Skow, William Waldron, and Dan Wilby.

➵ **Clients:** Peri and Nacho Arenas, Adam and Denise, Liz Lange, Nanette Lepore and Bob Savage, Stan Parker and Jennifer Deppe Parker, Doug Teitelbaum, and Barbie.

➵ **Family:** Amy, David, Harry, Mom, my late father, and my favorite person on earth, Simon.

➵ **Sterling operatives:** Marcus Leaver, Jason Prince, Joelle Herr, Ashley Prine, and Melissa McKoy.

➵ **JA peeps:** Fearless Leaders: Gary Fuhrman, Erik Baker, and David Frankel. Those who worked on the book: Stephen Moss, Leslie Degler, Jerin Tueck, and Edwin Vera, and a thank you to the entire JA team, from the warehouse, the stores, the office, and the design studio.

➵ **And, finally, to the group that slaved away to create this book: Celia Fuller, Pam Horn, Jen Renzi, and the sublime Charlotte Hillman.**

Library of Congress Cataloging-in-Publication Data Available

10 9 8 7 6 5 4 3 2 1

Published by Sterling Publishing Co., Inc.
387 Park Avenue South, New York, NY 10016
© 2010 by Jonathan Adler
Distributed in Canada by Sterling Publishing
c/o Canadian Manda Group, 165 Dufferin Street
Toronto, Ontario, Canada M6K 3H6
Distributed in the United Kingdom by
GMC Distribution Services
Castle Place, 166 High Street, Lewes, East Sussex,
England BN7 1XU
Distributed in Australia by
Capricorn Link (Australia) Pty. Ltd.
P.O. Box 704, Windsor, NSW 2756, Australia

Design by Celia Fuller
Cover photo © Ngoc Minh Ngo
Jonathan Adler Executive Editor: Charlotte Hillman

Sterling ISBN 978-1-4027-7431-7

For information about custom editions, special sales, premium and corporate purchases, please contact Sterling Special Sales Department at 800-805-5489 or specialsales@sterlingpublishing.com.

CONTENTS

Foreword *by Simon Doonan*   4

Introduction: Vanquish the Vanilla   6

TRUE BLUE   8

HELLO, YELLOW!   28

BLANC ⚘ NOIR   42

GOING ROUGE   56

CHAMBEIGE   74

ORANGE CRUSH   90

GANG GREEN   108

PRECIOUS METALS   124

Final Musings   138

Photo Credits   140

Index   141

➥ FOREWORD

Not long after I met Jonathan Adler, he was stricken with a hideous flu.

"Run to the video store and rent a movie that will transport me out of my misery," he demanded in a regal, **ROCK-STAR-ISH** way.

I proudly returned—remember VHS rentals?—clutching what I thought would be the ultimate distraction, a deliriously mesmerizing kaleidoscope of color, namely Federico Fellini's *Juliet of the Spirits.*

"You are simply not going to believe the colors!!!" I kvelled, popping the tape into the machine.

Jonathan's eyes rolled up into his head. He groaned loudly. "I spend my whole life obsessing about color combinations. Color is what I do for a living. I need something REALLY distracting. Like *The Terminator.*"

It is true. Jonathan's waking life has always been a nonstop tussle with swatches and chips, a veritable color **CAGE FIGHT.** He is always on the hunt for the next improbable color combo, the next mad magenta, the ultimate olive.

The **AGONY** of his obsession with color is, of course, far outweighed by the **ECSTASY** thereof. The intention of this book is to share that passion, the passion of Technicolor living, with you.

SIMON DOONAN

P.S. If you have never seen *Juliet of the Spirits,* give it a whirl.

⤳ INTRODUCTION:
VANQUISH THE VANILLA!

So many people shy away from using color in their homes for fear of getting it wrong. In a quest for tastefulnessness, they take the risk-averse route of avoidance, acquiescing to perfunctory, pallid hues and a paucity of pattern. But ignorance and fear are no reason to live in a bland box. Beige is a bummer! Colorless is characterless! So vanquish the vanilla: Bold colors will make you happy!

Yes, I know, decorating is hard stuff. Interior design is the ultimate contact sport; **IT IS NOT FOR SISSIES.** But I have developed a foolproof formula to help anyone achieve a resolved yet personal look. Working color into your decor is an art, but it's also a science—one with formulas and prescriptions that can be followed to achieve chromatic euphoria. The trick is to start with a solid foundation of good decorating—clean lines, classic elements—and then give it an irreverent tweak, injecting your own signature via kicky color and graphic punch.

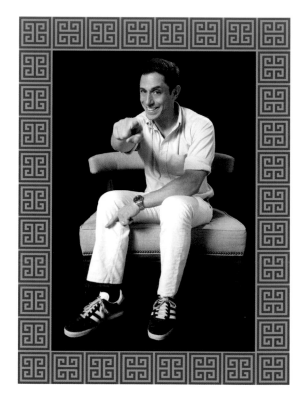

95% CHIC + 5% HAPPY = THE DECORATIVE NIRVANA THAT I CALL HAPPY CHIC

Everything you need to know to tackle your color-related design quandaries—whether choosing an accent color or divining the best way to weave brocade or paisley into your life—can be found in this tome.

Where to start? Your home should reflect who you are, so pick a palette that's close to your heart and run with it. I'll walk you through my own favorite colors to show you inspirational examples. Have a fondness for jaunty *jaunes*? Check out the chapter on yellow for guidance and inspiration. Want to check checks and geometrics off your to-do list? Included are numerous examples—from houndstooths to Greek keys—accompanied by tips and tricks.

Embrace chromatic exuberance through paint color, fabrics, pillows, and tchotchkes that are easily updated so your home can evolve happily and chicly with you.

LOVE WHAT
YOU LOVE!

TRUE BLUE

My first love was baby blue.

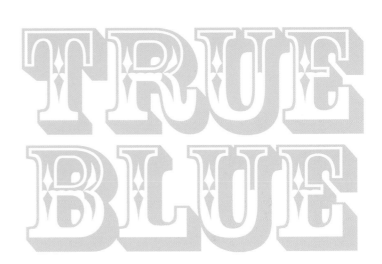

We have known each other my entire life, but I feel like I first saw baby blue—first really got to know her—in 1989. Madonna's Like a Prayer came out that year and the album cover (art directed by her fabulously talented and now estranged frère, Christopher) was a revelation to yours truly. Typical '80s Madonna fare: a close-up of her NUDE midsection, dripping with jewels, the top button of her jeans undone and promising more.

Whatever. The real KAPOW! of the cover was the graphic baby-blue starburst covering her navel. My God was that a baby blue! That Madonna baby blue has since been a cornerstone of my pottery, my textiles, my decorating, my everything.

But lately, my eye has begun to wander. I'm not proud of it, my twenty-year itch, but it happens. I've been cheating on baby blue with her sister, turquoise. And, I admit, I've had a little bit of an affair with TEAL. Okay, INDIGO too. And NAVY. Fine, I've been having a love affair with...the entire blue family! Lord, does it feel good to get that off my chest!

But I'm not a selfish lover. Au contraire. I encourage you, all of you, to join my love-pile and embrace blue in all her Happy Chic glory and iterations.

Repeat color accents for added impact. Here, black and white zigzags anchor intense bursts of turquoise throughout, lending the light and lively shade a bit of gravitas. Never shy from a secondary accent hue; in this room, a few well-placed touches of yellow add extra zest.

"Any color works if you push it to the extreme."
—MASSIMO VIGNELLI

Color continuity is the cornerstone of artful table-scaping. This composition of light blue and cobalt accessories coordinates with the painting above (a portrait of my beloved Norwich terrier, Liberace). A glint of silver glams it up a notch!

MOD UP YOUR SOFA, BED, SHELF, OR WINDOW SEAT WITH COLOR AND PATTERN VIA GRANNY-GONE-WILD NEEDLEPOINT PILLOWS!

BLENDING BLUES

This seating area in my New York apartment demonstrates the dictum that multiple shades of blue always work harmoniously together. Create spatial continuity simply by repeating colors. The navy upholstery picks up the lighter sky blue of the zig-zag carpet, while the Ed Paschke painting of Sly Stone brings the hue up the wall. Keeping colors consistent elevates this vignette into a room-within-a-room.

The stairwell leading to my man-boudoir is lined floor-to-ceiling in super-trippy blue hexagons. The retro geometrics are courtesy of David Hicks, one of my heroes. The buttoned-up blue tempers the silvery foil background of the wallpaper so it doesn't look too bling. The metallic sheen also opens up the dark space.

HEXAGONS CREATE ONE OF MY FAVORITE PATTERNS; I LOVE THE COMBINATION OF GEOMETRIC RIGOR AND DYNAMISM THEY IMPART.

MINI **MUSE**:
HALSTON

Every morning when I walk downstairs, I catch of glimpse of Roxanne Lowit's iconic photo of Halston. The designer and *bon vivant* is one of my inspirational muses—a funster of yore whom I consider a spiritual ancestor. He had the modernity and ability to fuse socialite chic with suggestions of high-flying decadence that I aspire to achieve in my own oeuvre.

GO BATTY FOR **Blue!**

- *Wear white jeans with a **denim** shirt.*

- *Punctuate your pad with **turquoise** lacquer cube tables.*

- *Put **Anne Slater**–style blue lenses in your eyeglasses.*

- *Make **blueberry** shortcake.*

- *Fill blue enamel bowls with **cobalt M&Ms**.*

- *Go for a swim in an **aquamarine pool**.*

MIXING BLUE

Blue is a versatile design tool; it gets along swimmingly with so many other shades. Here are some of my favorite combos:

BENJAMIN MOORE
••••••••••
TRUE BLUE
2066-50

+

BENJAMIN MOORE
••••••••••
EVENING BLUE
2066-20

+

BENJAMIN MOORE
••••••••••
BLUE LAPIS
2067-40

WHEN IN DOUBT: *Blue* **+ blue + blue.** Choose a festival of blues—turquoise mixed with navy mixed with azure mixed with baby blue.

CHIC AND CLASSIQUE: *Baby blue* **+ chocolate brown** is one of my favorite combos. It's both tasteful and deluxe.

BENJAMIN MOORE
••••••••••
LIGHT BLUE
2066-20

+

BENJAMIN MOORE
••••••••••
MINK
2112-10

TRICKY TREAT: *Blue* **+ yellow.** Keep one color soft, the other one punchy; when both hues are bright, the effect is too loud.

BENJAMIN MOORE
••••••••••
EVENING BLUE
2066-20

+

BENJAMIN MOORE
••••••••••
LEMON MERINGUE
2023-50

YOU CAN'T GO WRONG WITH BLUE AND WHITE

Turquoise makes a captivating accent color and is especially sassy when set against a white background. Curtains are an effortless way to bring color into a space—and simple to swap when you yearn for a fresh look.

USE ACCESSORIES TO ECHO THE COLORS OF SURROUNDING FABRICS.

DEMI LUNE TABLES ARE PERFECT LITTLE SPACE FILLERS.

AN ODE TO

GLASS

Translucent glass brings sparkling wit to any room. Exploit the material's light-catching property by lining a windowsill with it or—counterintuitively—placing it in a dark corner to invite illumination. Glass is an ideal accent for wet areas like the bathroom, where moisture limits your materials options.

The easiest, happiest solution to any sad and lonely shelf? Poppy glass bottles from The End of History (theendofhistoryshop.blogspot.com), my go-to resource. This New York City vintage shop sells an inspired rainbow of brightly colored glass—all organized and displayed by hue.

BLUE-SPIRATION!

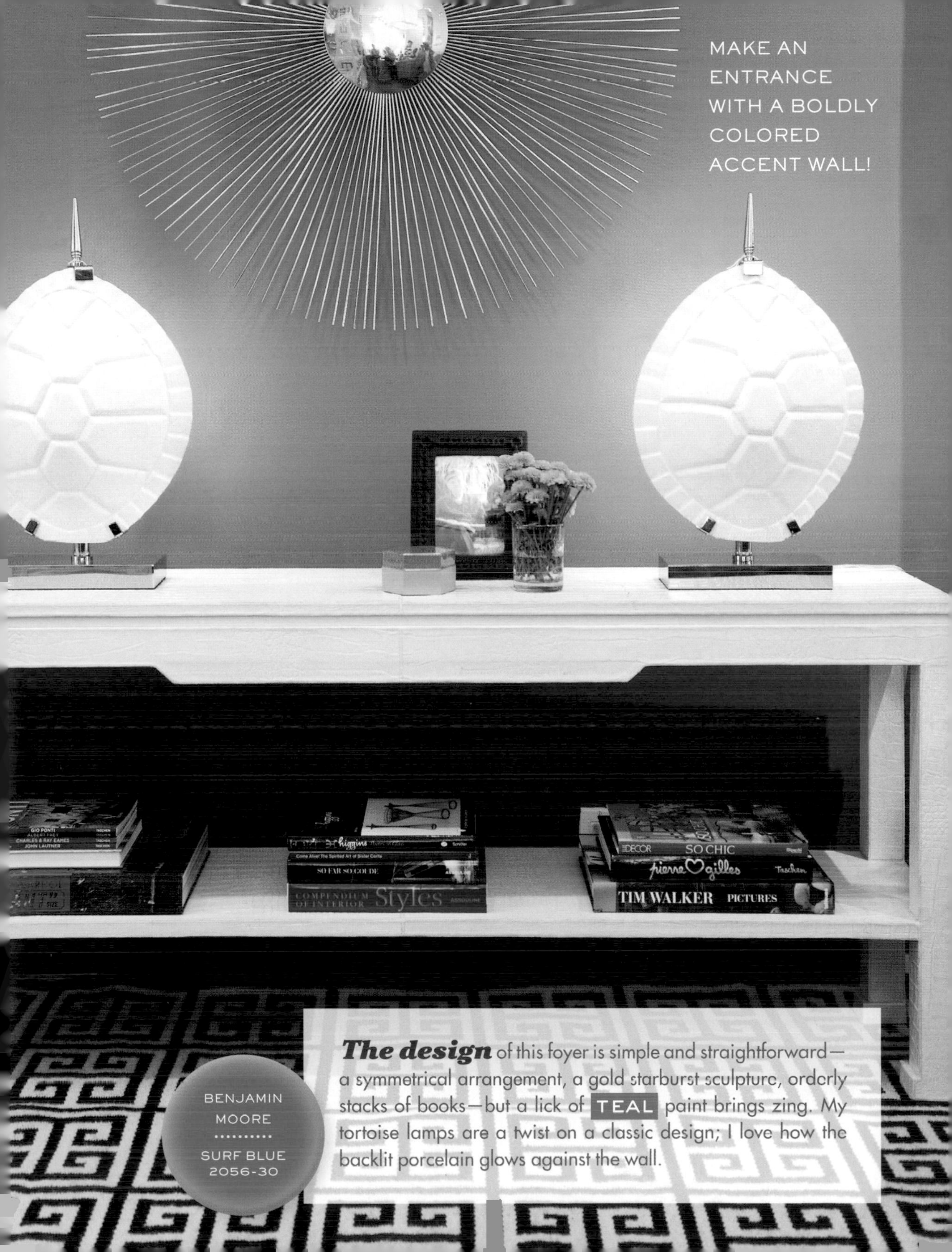
GIO PONTI
ALBERT FREY
CHARLES & RAY EAMES
JOHN LAUTNER
TASCHEN
higgins
SO FAR SO GOUDE
COMPENDIUM OF INTERIOR Styles
DECOR
SO CHIC
pierre gilles
Taschen
TIM WALKER PICTURES

MAKE AN ENTRANCE WITH A BOLDLY COLORED ACCENT WALL!

BENJAMIN MOORE

SURF BLUE 2056-30

The design of this foyer is simple and straightforward—a symmetrical arrangement, a gold starburst sculpture, orderly stacks of books—but a lick of TEAL paint brings zing. My tortoise lamps are a twist on a classic design; I love how the backlit porcelain glows against the wall.

A blue striped runner draws your eye to the eclectic vignette at the far end of this hallway. The lacquered orange planter, organic carved-wood chair by Wendell Castle, and Venetian mirror provide a foretaste of the colorful fun to be had in the adjoining room.

Don't overlook stair risers!
I added nautical flair to this back stairway by painting the risers in tones of blue. The rope railing gives an extra **"AHOY."**

MU$e

Gio Ponti's Hotel Parco dei Principi

When you think of blue, you probably think of the sea or the sky, but you should really think of the Parco dei Principi Hotel in Sorrento, Italy. Gio Ponti's masterwork makes the sea and the sky seem like amateurish attempts to harness the sublime **POWER OF BLUE.** Cerulean, azure, turquoise, cobalt, indigo, and teal all mingle and riff and have a party, proving that when it comes to blues, the more the merrier.

Perched on a cliff in Sorrento overlooking the Gulf of Naples, the hotel's 96 guest rooms and the epic and inspiring public areas are like a watercolor paean to the surrounding sea. Painted ceramic tiles are everywhere—walls, floors, ceilings— and they are mesmerizing. Ponti limited the patterns in the hotel to just three simple graphics, but **TWEAKED** and **TWISTED** the layouts to achieve seemingly limitless variations.

Ponti was a **FEARLESS** designer—bold, brash, brimming with bravado—and there is no better example than the Parco dei Principi. I strongly advise you to put down this book immediately, head straight to the airport, fly to Sorrento, check into the hotel, and never leave.

HELLO, YELLOW!

If I were a doctor, *I would prescribe yellow to cure all ills. I'd write a proper prescription (in illegible handwriting, of course) and send it to a magical pharmacist who could create a special potion—in the form of a color swatch—for any malady.* STOMACH FLU? *A bracing lemon yellow.* BROKEN HEART? *The happy gold of Samantha's flaxen hair on* Bewitched. A.D.D.? *A soothing egg yolk.* HEADACHE? *The yellow of Jan Brady's sweet sixteen shift. Just stare at the swatch and* voilà: *all better! So, go on, take two doses of* CANARY YELLOW *and call me in the morning.*

Alas, I'm not a proper doctor. But I do believe that yellow has healing properties. It's simply impossible not to feel good when eating a Marshmallow Peep or chewing a stick of lemon-flavored Fruit Stripe gum. Yellow equals Happy Chic joie de vivre *and* SUNNY *optimism.*

Why not surround a blue ping-pong table with yellow stadium seating? A ping-pong table is essential to your mental health and well being; playing the game is the ultimate stress reducer. It is a must-have item of furniture for any aspiring funster.

"Yellow is capable of charming God."

—VINCENT VAN GOGH

MINI **Muse**: EMILIO PUCCI

Everything you need to know about mixing crazy colors can be gleaned from Pucci prints. The '60s designer was all about multicolored fabrics with psychedelic stripes and swirly swooshes. Emilio Pucci was a genius at mixing seemingly discordant hues like purple and puce and pink. His trick was to use colors of the same value, punctuated with an **ELECTRIC** note. For an instant palette to guide your decor, just take a fabric swatch and match two or three stripes to Benjamin Moore paint chips.

Conventional (read: bo-ring!) decorating wisdom would suggest picking dining chairs to match the luminous draperies. But all-turquoise here would have looked too decorator-y and trad, so here in Liz Lange's country house, we played against type by throwing in a wild card: Chippendale chairs in shocking lemony yellow. Unusual color combinations are so much more effective than the expected matchy-matchy standbys.

YELLOW-SPIRATION!

JIM THOMPSON

YELLOW

IS THE LEMON SORBET OF THE HOME.

YELLOW NIRVANA!

LACHAPELLE

KOONS

SEX OBSESSIONS

The Big Penis Book

TASCHEN

UHLAMS

HELMUT NEWTON

VANITY FAIR PORTRAITS

Richard AvEdoN

DAVID LACHAPELLE

ADD SASS WITH
CITRON SEATS.

PEACE OUT
WITH A COBALT
THROW PILLOW
AGAINST MUSTARD
UPHOLSTERY!

BELLOW FOR
Yellow

- *Light up your life:* Make a window shade from daffodil-yellow linen.

- *Frame Andy Warhol's iconic Velvet Underground album cover of a big* **banana** *and hang it above the toilet.*

- *One yellow Gerber daisy in a bud vase =* **Prozac** *for your pad.*

- *Every kitchen needs a* **mound of lemons.**

- *Tie a* **yellow ribbon** *'round…your neck for a summer picnic.*

- *Keep your secret life a secret inside a* **bright yellow** *monogrammed Goyard agenda.*

- *Treat yourself to some* **Marshmallow Peeps**— *you know you love them.*

- *Wear something* **chrome yellow** *at night. You don't want to end up as roadkill!*

MIXING YELLOW

WHEN IN DOUBT:
Yellow + **gray.**
Tone down yellow's brash sunniness with sedate gray for a soothing '40s feel. You can't go wrong with this duo—any shades will work.

BENJAMIN MOORE
....
SUN PORCH
2023-30

BENJAMIN MOORE
....
WOLF GRAY
2127-40

BENJAMIN MOORE
....
BABY CHICK
2023-20

BENJAMIN MOORE
....
SPRING MOSS
2027-20

CHIC AND CLASSIQUE:
Yellow + **green.**
This zesty pairing is a one-way ticket to Palm Beach.

TRICKY TREAT:
Yellow + **black.**
Keep it from reading "bumblebee" by letting black and white predominate and spooning in just a soupçon of yellow.

BENJAMIN MOORE
....
BRIGHT YELLOW
2022-30

BENJAMIN MOORE
....
JET BLACK
2120-10

MUSE

The Isle of Capri

I'm not a very adventurous traveler. You won't find me stalking rhinos in Uganda. Maybe I'm just an old fart, but if I go somewhere and have a fab time, then I go back. My CAUTIOUS JEWISH GENE has made me a creature of habit.

One place where I have *had a fab time*—AGAIN and AGAIN and AGAIN—*is Capri. The island is so totally '50s. It looks and feels exactly the way it did in* The Talented Mr. Ripley *and Godard's* Contempt. *(My bloke, Simon, and I have been obsessed with the freaky mod beauty of Casa Malaparte ever since we saw it in* Contempt; *we are forever hanging around the front gate hoping a nice Caprese cleaning lady will let us in so we can snoop around.) For further insight into the* SURREAL GLAMOUR *of Capri, rent* Boom!, *the 1968 Tennessee Williams movie starring Elizabeth Taylor and Richard Burton. Terrible film, but the decor of Liz Taylor's compound is perfection!*

Whenever in Capri, I stay at LA SCALINATELLA. *Sublime and surprising, La Scalinatella is heaven on earth! The lobby—with its tile floors, clover-shaped windows, and surreal objects—perfectly captures the dreamy quality of Capri. I love that each object, whether a '60s ceramic stool shaped like a tassel or a gilded Baroque mirror, is carefully selected, beautiful, and* IMPROBABLE. *I think about the lobby often while designing interiors; La Scalinatella's surreal spirit is inspiring and liberating.*

BLANC and NOIR

I have a soft spot for the crisp pairing of black and white. In fact, I started my career making black-and-white-striped pots. My inspiration was **THE GRADUATE**—notably the black-and-white striped awning in Mrs. Robinson's backyard. It was so smart, so sharp, so country club chic! Awning stripes say everything that needs to be said about black and white: nifty, **POPPY,** punchy perfection. Think Geoffrey Beene. Slim Aarons. Irving Penn. Horst P. Horst. **THINK VANS!**

You simply cannot go wrong expressing yourself in black and white; it's a fail-safe pairing that's graphic yet neutral and impossible to screw up.

It's either black and white or just white. I wear white pants every single day, even to black-tie events. When it comes to attiring your home, however, it's best to use white as a neutral backdrop for exuberant colors rather than as a statement in and of itself; white on white is so cold and antiseptic looking (and yet, ironically, so impossible to keep clean). In its previous incarnation, my New York apartment featured every color under the moon. Then I tore off the grass cloth wallpaper and jettisoned the jolly accent walls and whitewashed every available surface. The result? Everything **POPPED.** White lets Happy Chic colors be themselves.

White is the ultimate soothing backdrop; just be sure to pick paint with the subtlest touch of cream and a matte, rather than glossy, finish so it's not too stark. Although I typically favor white as a primer for high-octane hues, it can look equally tasteful paired with muted tones like ethereal gray and blue—a palette that makes this dressing room feel like the swishiest hotel in the world.

HIGH-RELIEF MOLDINGS GIVE SPARE, MODERN ARCHITECTURE INSTANT PATINA AND A TOP NOTE OF NEOCLASSICAL SWANK.

MIXING BLACK AND WHITE

BENJAMIN MOORE
·········
UNIVERSAL BLACK
2118-10

+

BENJAMIN MOORE
·········
ICE MIST
OC-67

+

BENJAMIN MOORE
·········
SURF BLUE
2056-30

WHEN IN DOUBT: **Black** + *white* + *turquoise.* This spirited shade of blue has enough brio to hold its own against the assertiveness of *blanc* and *noir.*

BENJAMIN MOORE
·········
SPACE BLACK
2119-10

+

BENJAMIN MOORE
·········
SNOW WHITE
OC-66

+

BENJAMIN MOORE
·········
METALLIC SILVER
2132-60

CHIC AND CLASSIQUE: **Black** + *white* + *silver.* Enhanced with a slick of shine, the look is bold and a little fancy.

BENJAMIN MOORE
·········
BLACK IRON
2120-20

+

BENJAMIN MOORE
·········
PURE WHITE
OC-64

+

BENJAMIN MOORE
·········
BROWN SUGAR
2112-20

TRICKY TREAT: **Black** + *white* + **brown.** This rustic look says, "I know I'm breaking the rules—but I don't care!" The key: the brown should come from natural textures like leather, wood, or nubby linen.

MINI MU**S**e: DOROTHY DRAPER

She was the queen of creating architectural rigor via purely decorative touches: elaborate moldings, punchy cabbage prints, wild wallpapers. Her oeuvre was at once overbold and totally disciplined. The secret to her **KAPOW** style? A reliance on crisp, contrasty hues—black and white among them—provided a framework for her exuberance, which culminated in her legendary designs for the Greenbrier Resort and the Carlyle Hotel.

Black AND White
BLISS

◆ *White tablecloths + black napkins = **Op Art** minus linty crotches!*

◆ *Put a white skunk stripe in your black hair. **Think Daphne Guinness.***

◆ *Embrace the majesty of a **faux-zebra rug.***

◆ *Buy vintage **Courrèges scarves** on eBay and make pillows.*

◆ ***Checkerboard Vans** are forever.*

◆ ***Budget-conscious glamour-seekers:** Hand-paint black stripes in a white room using a one-inch foam brush.*

◆ *For an intellectual look, try a black flat-front pant with a **crisp white shirt.** (Buddy Holly eyewear optional.)*

◆ *Fill a big white bowl with black **marble eggs.***

SURRENDER TO THE
GLAMOUR OF
WHITE

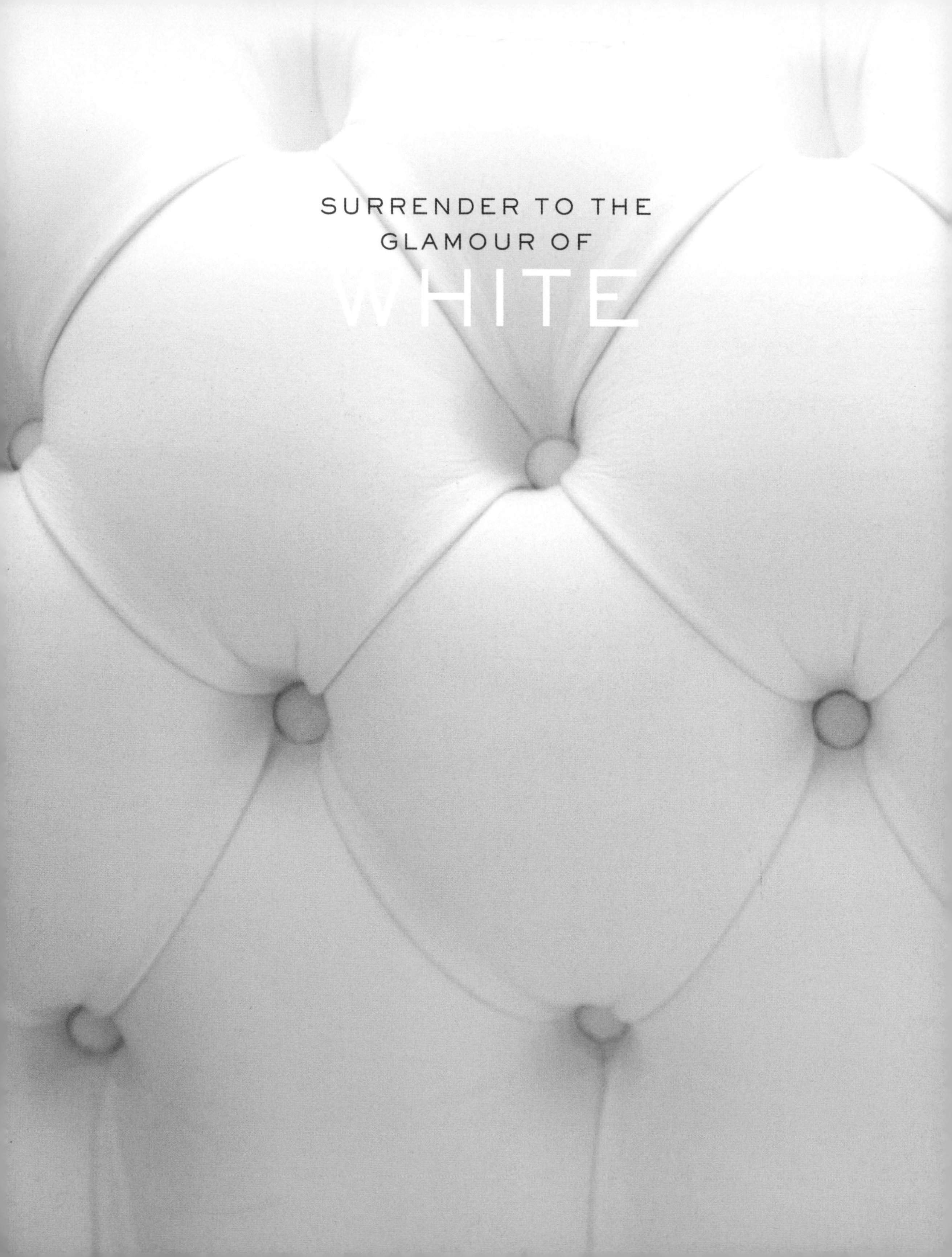

This is my needlepoint tribute to Rudi Gernreich's muse and collaborator, the mod queen of black and white. Making waves in the designer's topless maillot, La Moffitt embodied all that was sexy and swinging about the '60s.

Grandma chic goes groovy.
Verner Panton's mod black-and-white Geometri fabric, a '60s design, makes even a classic Louis *chaise* look modern.

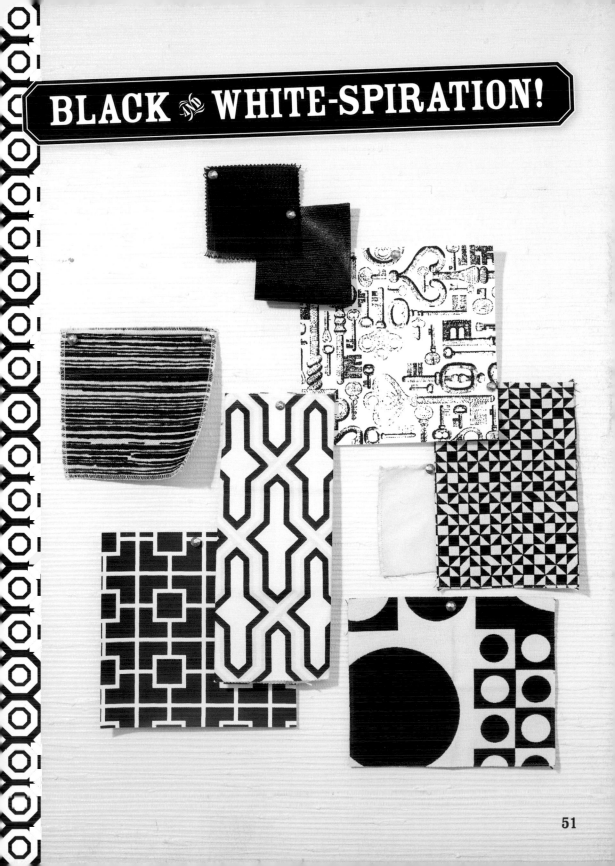

BLACK AND WHITE-SPIRATION!

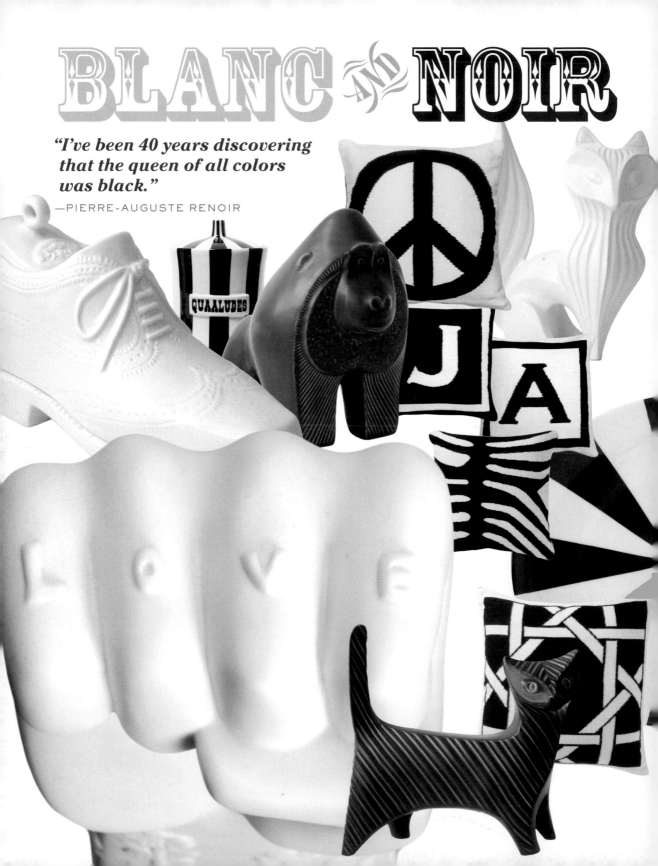

BLANC AND NOIR

"I've been 40 years discovering that the queen of all colors was black."

—PIERRE-AUGUSTE RENOIR

MUSE

Fornasetti

Piero Fornasetti—patriarch of the Fornasetti design house— had a singular vision but myriad talents. He was a creative polymath in the way that only Italians can be. Fornasetti was a decorator, a ceramicist, a painter, a scenarist, a designer of furniture, products, and textiles, and much, much more.

To me, though, he is the embodiment of irreverent luxury. His favorite trick was to take an archetypal piece of furniture—many designed by his son, Barnaba—and decorate it using his sophisticated printing technique with an image of something dissonant. To take a perfect piece and add a little something extra, a decorative appliqué, is what Happy Chic is all about. His work is a reminder to embrace the QUIRKY, *the* SURREAL, *and the* UNINHIBITED. *And he reminds me to deface furniture. To Fornasetti nothing was sacred, and everything could use an extra something!*

Fornasetti was also a master at witty and improbable juxtapositions, turning a chair back into a woman's torso or a giant Corinthian column. Everything he designed, whether a wallpaper pattern or a folding screen, winks back at you. Sometimes almost literally, as in the case of a china plate he decorated with a lady's come-hither face. This is another reason why he is my muse: Fornasetti applied faces—my favorite motif—to his products. Not that he didn't love a little backside*, too. Fornasetti was Italian, after all.

(*For Italian design with a naughty side, see also: Carlo Mollino.)

GOING ROUGE

Red is a dangerous color! *Think of the peek-a-boo sole of a Christian Louboutin stiletto, the lipstick pout of neo-burlesque diva* **DITA VON TEESE,** *or* Sex and the City*'s Mr. Big painting his bedroom wall a flaming* rouge *as a symbol of* après-le-divorce *liberation. Riveting* **RED** *equals passion and temptation. For proof, look no further than Eve in the Garden of Eden, taking a delicious bite of a big, juicy apple. Red is a loaded gun: a great weapon to have at your disposal, but one to use for Happy Chic good rather than evil.*

*   **PINK,** red's wayward little sister, is just fun! There's nothing dangerous about pretty pink—except when it comes to picking the proper shade. Pure pink is too cloying; a hint of gray or lavender tempers the saccharine froth. Apply judiciously rather than liberally, lest you risk a slap-happy sugar rush, and pair with less emotive hues. Just a pop of pink, or it looks too* **PAH-ZINK.**

Pink predominates.

Little pink accents—floral fabric, a Union Jack chair pillow—give this room Carnaby Street spice.

Eero Saarinen's Tulip chair is pure genius, able to mix well with almost any style or design genre. Since its 1955 debut, nothing has one-upped it.

CLEAR LUCITE KNOBS MAKE EVERYTHING FEEL SO MUCH MORE COUTURE. I USE THEM ALL OVER MY HOUSE, FROM DRAWER PULLS TO DOORKNOBS.

Use an allover mural-like wallpaper to electrify a jewel box of a loo. It's impossible to go overboard with color or pattern in a small space.

RED-SPIRATION!

MAGENTA = A TINGLING SENSATION IN ALL YOUR CHAKRAS

61

MINI **MUSE**: BARBIE

Barbie is a somewhat controversial American icon whom some dismiss as fluff, but I choose to see her as a symbol of female empowerment—and proof of the power of PINK. Sometimes what we perceive as superficial and lighthearted is actually quite subversive and strong.

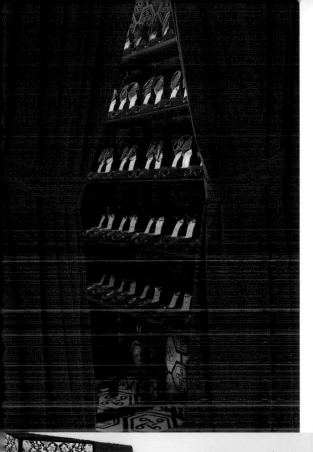

I was recently tapped to design a house as part of Barbie's fiftieth birthday celebration. We took over a Malibu manse and furnished it soup to nuts—from table settings to the shoe closet—as if a real-life Barbie lived there. The project was very self-referential, with furniture fashioned from actual Barbie dolls and lots of playful dressmaker details like tutus and pleats. Real-life clients can be such a drag—all about storage and practicality—so Barbie was a breath of fresh air. And, luckily, there was no husband around to rein in the glamour or tone down the pink.

HAVE A HOT, SPICY
AFFAIR WITH REBEL

RED

Racy red packs a punch on
this needlepoint power pillow.

65

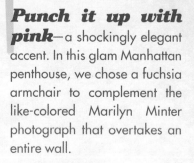

Punch it up with pink—a shockingly elegant accent. In this glam Manhattan penthouse, we chose a fuchsia armchair to complement the like-colored Marilyn Minter photograph that overtakes an entire wall.

Skinny stripes pull together disparate colors, keeping the look sharp and not dizzying. This pinstriped fabric vacillates between `RED` and `PINK` thanks to thin bands of both, interspersed with purple and blue.

My bloke and I have a weird Juliet balcony overlooking our double-height living room, which is presided over by artist Claire Zeisler's offbeat sculpture. A giant red string ball is very Happy Chic.

My ping-pong table is made from a slab of plywood affixed to Saarinen Tulip table bases and wallpapered in red paisley. I made it myself, but with much hardship and woe; it took several tries and a lot of off-color commentary to get it right. Do not try this at home unless you are married to a carpenter. Save yourself the trouble and customize a standard ping-pong table with fun wallpaper.

PAISLEY LENDS EXOTIC ALLURE TO ANY ROOM.

Our New York living room was very underutilized — just a sad annex to the TV den — until it was reborn as a game room. I cleared out the furniture and plopped a ping-pong table smack in the middle. There's nothing better at the end of a day than whacking a ping-ping ball with (or at) your better half.

LITTLE Red STYLING TIPS

✦ *Glamorize your debts:* *Keep your unpaid bills in a red-lacquered box.*

✦ *Make a small room more important:* *Paint your laundry room, closet, or powder room blood red.*

✦ *Delude yourself that* *red velvet cupcakes* *are healthier and less fattening than regular ones.*

✦ *Give yourself a legal high with a* *burgundy Moroccan pouf.*

✦ *Take a cue from Prince: Buy yourself a raspberry beret.*

✦ *Stay ahead of the curve: Rediscover the* *Maraschino cherry* *before anyone else does.*

MIXING ROUGE

BENJAMIN MOORE
....
MILLION DOLLAR RED 2003-10

BENJAMIN MOORE
....
MINK 2112-10

WHEN IN DOUBT: *Red* + *brown.* This fail-safe complement is unexpected—yet unimpeachable.

BENJAMIN MOORE
....
RED 2000-10

BENJAMIN MOORE
....
DECORATOR'S WHITE

BENJAMIN MOORE
....
ADMIRAL BLUE 2065-10

CHIC AND CLASSIQUE: *Red* + *white* + *blue.* Not just for the Fourth of July, this feel-good American staple should be enjoyed year-round.

BENJAMIN MOORE
....
SMOLDERING RED 2007-10

BENJAMIN MOORE
....
YELLOW OXIDE 2154-10

TRICKY TREAT: *Red* + *gold.* It can go lurid, so curate with care.

To make red and gold work, keep the gold a little burnished, choose a red with a bit of gloss, and layer in plenty of white space for visual breathing room. Here, the unusual color pairing emphasizes the mash-up of genres—the juxtaposition of a Rococo mirror and a Ron Arad club chair—while the curvy profiles draw out their similarities.

MUSE

Diana Vreeland

Every third sentence out of my mouth is a Diana Vreeland quote. Consider these bon mots:

"Too much good taste can be boring."

"Pink is the navy blue of India."

"I loathe narcissism, but I approve of vanity."

"Brigitte Bardot's lips made Mick Jagger's lips possible."

If you've spent any time around me, you might assume that these clever witticisms are my own, so often do they spring forth from my lips. But I like to give credit where credit is due, and a large percentage of my vocabulary is courtesy of the ever-quotable La Vreeland.

Yes, yes; I know it's a cliché to say Diana Vreeland is your muse. What designer/decorator/fashionista hasn't she inspired? She is the muse to end all muses. And to top it all off, she lived in a Park Avenue lair designed by Billy Baldwin that had a living room lacquered bright, bright red. RESPECT.

CHAM-BEIGE

I am a firm believer in neutrals *to anchor bright pops of color; a neutral palette lets you go batty with hyperbolic hues and unapologetic pattern. But the word "neutral" sounds so snoozy, so I coined a new phrase for it:* **CHAMBEIGE,** *Which is just what it sounds like: beige with a buzz.* **DRINK UP!**

As a potter, I've always had a soft spot for the honest expression of natural materials. Clay is all about mosses, dusks, and terra cotta. The best neutrals are natural elements in their raw state. Mother Earth favors the chambeiges of the world, so revel in the gorgeous Happy Chic majesty of mundane materials: let linen be oatmeal-colored, let wood be reddish brown, let bronze be bronze, let concrete be Brutalist gray.

As much as I love bold color, I am also a strong believer in letting materials be what they are.

Replete with rich natural materials, this open-plan living space is a study in eclecticism. Chambeige hues and textured elements conspire to create lyrical organicism: unstained wide-plank floors, sisal carpeting, oatmeal linen drapes, and whitewashed walls and ceiling with wood grain peeking through. All the finishes are an honest expression of their true nature: I let wood be wood, chrome be chrome, and iron be iron so that the effect doesn't feel stark.

MINI *Muse*:
THE POST RANCH INN

Post Ranch Inn in Big Sur, California, is cham-beige heaven. The decor is rustic and lovely but plays second fiddle to the main attraction: the views! There is nothing more sublime than waking up and seeing the spectacular cliff-top vistas. Big Sur is my favorite place on earth, and the Post Ranch Inn has just the right sense of place. The design lets the natural beauty—rather than the architecture—dominate.

CHAMBEIGE

IS NOT A COLOR—IT'S A STATE OF MIND!

CHAMBEIGE
CAN SWING HIPPIE,
TRADITIONAL, OR
GENTLEMANLY
DEPENDING
ON HOW YOU
SPIN IT.

✚ Choose ethnic touches to bring color and pattern to a space. This rug, a pieced-together Oriental patchwork, exudes clubby-English-gone-modern appeal.

CHAMBEIGE-SPIRATION!

Let materials speak for themselves. A wood wall creates a sense of rustic luxury, while the French '50s mirrors are an unexpected scale over the sink.

LET COLOR COME FROM NATURAL MATERIALS IN UNADULTERATED STATES, LIKE UNSTAINED WOOD.

PUT IT IN **Neutral**

◆ *Surrender to the Zen of grass cloth. Cover the wall behind your bed.*

◆ *Snag a caramel-colored Chesterfield and learn to vault over the back.*

◆ *Experience Nakashima.*

◆ *Take a macramé class.*

◆ *Rent a house at the Sea Ranch modern hippie community in California.*

◆ *Build an outdoor shower using bamboo fencing and locust posts.*

◆ *Support the craftspeople of the world: Wear a Peruvian poncho next winter.*

Clay is the chambeigiest material in the world, so as a potter I will always have a love affair with natural colors and textures. The ultimate chambeige accessory is Liberace!

Here, we rocked a bit

of louche glamour with a Halston-esque padded leather built-in platform, gray ultrasuede walls, and butterscotch leather upholstery. Platforms—an old Paul Rudolph trick that reached its apex during the High Tech trend of the '70s—have (sadly) fallen out of favor, but platforms are a great way to create dynamism and demarcate space.

The many moods of chambeige.

The color scheme of this New York bachelor pad is neutral, but the content of the objects is anything but: racy Terry Richardson photos, Philippe Starck gun lamps, a witty trio of chrome side tables. It's the rebellious side of chambeige.

GLAMOU

MUSe

Sheila Hicks

➥ *She is a Fiber Revolutionary who elevated a stereotypically "female" craft into high art.*

➥ *Inspired by Peruvian and Mexican textile traditions, she interweaves Latin-American inspirations and Minimalist art sensibility to create a super groovy product.*

➥ *She makes the most basic stuff—yarn—into unexpected and beautiful configurations through simple techniques like knitting, felting, and twisting.*

➥ *She is a Yale MFA-trained artist who studied under color theorist Josef Albers, which could account for her* **TRIPPY,** *saturated palette.*

➥ *She makes large-scale, environmental pieces—including a wall hanging that incorporates* **FIVE TONS** *of linen thread—that blur the boundaries between architecture, decoration, and art.*

➥ *She practices the art of cognitive dissonance, utilizing soft materials to create surprisingly hard geometries.*

➥ *She makes the traditionally* **HIPPIE-DIPPIE** *medium—which walks the fine line between craft and art—seem serious. As a potter, I dig fellow craftspeople getting their propers!*

ORANGE CRUSH

Orange is the most controversial of colors. Many consider it to be the GAUCHE legacy of the freewheeling '70s. But what an unfair reputation that decade has! To me, the '70s were when the counterculture became the popular culture—and when adults finally felt liberated to EMBRACE IMMATURITY. You could be young again without having to be innocent! Orange shouted out to the world that you didn't take things too seriously: that you weren't old and crusty, that you were not your parents, and that you didn't have a living room full of plastic-covered furniture. Rather, your furniture was made of plastic—and it was probably designed by VERNER PANTON.

Diss orange at your own expense. Orange says, "I'm fun!" Use it to draw out your inner child: grab a FANTA and an orange Tootsie Pop and feel your Happy Chic life expand.

91

*My cozy New York den is a design
lab where I test out my latest cre-
ations—as well as unorthodox
color combinations. Here's how I
made* **BROWN** *and* **ORANGE**
work together:

➤ *A bold orange sofa sets the tone
and anchors the room.*

➤ *The intensity of the sofa is echoed by
the equally intense patterned lampshades, bold artworks, graphic rug,
and kicky throw pillows.*

➤ *Orange accent pieces on the coffee
and side tables—including lacquered trays and boxes—bounce
around the color.*

➤ *Animals make for a happy menag-
erie: greyhounds, horses, bulls,
snails, gazelles, birds, and a leather
rhino footstool.*

I went with a very curated vibe for the master bedroom of an urbane art collector. There are a lot of fancy people in here: John Lautner (wall sconces), Mattia Bonetti (side tables), Nan Goldin (photographs). The centerpiece, though, is an orange "head" sofa and cheeky pillows by the brilliant French conceptual artist Nicola L., known for her figurative furniture. A white and gold palette keeps everything serene. The room is grounded by a white Kyle Bunting cowhide carpet—very unexpected in a wall-to-wall format—and a Charles Hollis Jones Lucite bed with luxe gold accents.

In the same townhouse, a little girl's room is given playful punctuation by another figurative furnishing: Eero Aarnio's cartoony Pony chair in bright orange.

KIDS' IMAGINATIONS THRIVE IN OVER-DECORATED ROOMS.

In Simon's closet, an orange Chippendale chair glows gorgeously against a baby-blue background. A black-and-white pillow channels swingy '60s style.

MIX NG ORANGE

BENJAMIN
MOORE
·········
OUTRAGEOUS
ORANGE
2013-10

BENJAMIN
MOORE
·········
FESTIVE
ORANGE
2014-10

BENJAMIN
MOORE
·········
ELECTRIC
ORANGE
2015-10

BENJAMIN
MOORE
·········
OLD NAVY
2063-10

BENJAMIN
MOORE
·········
ANCHOR GRAY
2126-30

BENJAMIN
MOORE
·········
DEEP TAUPE
2111-10

WHEN IN DOUBT:

Orange + *navy.* There's something innately preppy about this combination.

CHIC AND CLASSIQUE:

Orange + *charcoal* lends a French '40s feel— very Jean-Michel Frank. It's the best of both worlds: impertinence with a little gravitas.

TRICKY TREAT:

Orange + *brown,* a cool combo that runs the risk of looking too dated. If you find yourself veering a bit *Three's Company,* stop! Think Hermès instead.

My bloke, Simon, is my floral muse. He wears a natty Liberty print shirt almost every day of the week. Here he is in his closet, surrounded by his sartorial splendor. Although I tend to shy away from flower motifs in interiors—I find them so, well, *flowery*—seeing him wear blossoms with such aplomb inspires me to work them in every now and again.

ORANGE-SPIRATION!

HOLLAND & S...

HUNT LEATHER CO

ORANGE =
ELECTROLYTES FOR
YOUR EYEBALLS.

For our bedroom, I chose a palette of blue and brown livened with strong pops of orange. The classic Scalamandré brocade looks modern when executed in orange and white. I love this fabric so much that I used it everywhere: to create lampshades, to upholster chairs, as door panels, and to pad the wall behind the bed.

Orange
YOU GLAD...

✦ *Orange* looks like happiness.

✦ *Orange* looks zesty with white.

✦ *Orange* looks magical on a *Hare Krishna.*

✦ *Orange* looks like sand feels on your feet.

✦ *Orange* looks **chic** with pink.

✦ *Orange* looks like Acapulco in the '60s.

✦ *Orange* looks like *Rajasthan* any time.

✦ *Orange* looks like *Astrud Gilberto* sounds.

✦ *Orange* looks like you're living the *California dream.*

⬡ Traditional patterns—such as brocade—when used in a bold color—like orange—seem miles more modern.

ORANGE AND PINK ARE FAR FANCIER THAN YOU THINK.

ORANGE

LOOKS AS CRISP AND REFRESHING AS IT TASTES.

103

My dining room is a celebration of l'orange, from the lacquered planters to the zigzag carpet and glass face sculptures on the mantel. Lots of white space gives ample breathing room. Other tricks for creating balance:

➥ Blue is the main accent color. A dab on either side wall balances things out and establishes symmetry.

➥ The repetition of circular motifs (the artwork, the globe lights, and the round chairs) softens the zigzag.

➥ Sunflowers provide a happy focal point.

➥ Perfect paint: Benjamin Moore white Marine Deck paint always looks amazing on floors.

BENJAMIN MOORE
·············
MARINE DECK

MU**S**e

India *is all about saturated hues that the Color Police would have you believe lawlessly clash: orange with pink, pink with purple, purple with mauve and a jolt of* SAFFRON. *The Indian culture is rich in color. Happy hues and exuberant expressionism seem to have suffused the collective unconscious. Even their neutrals are vibrant and shocking; in the words of another muse, the inimitable Diana Vreeland, "Pink is the navy blue of India."*

The Indian approach to color is so much more fun. A trip to TECHNICOLOR *Jaipur—nicknamed the Pink City—makes you realize that we are living needlessly boring black-and-white lives. Even the palace, Hawa Mahal, is pink! The truth of it is that color-loving India makes the rest of us seem like tepid, pathetic wusses. Our color sense has somehow been beaten into submission. Our ego would be much happier if our primal color id were allowed to run wild.*

GANG GREEN

Mother Nature has been good to us. *She's given us sleek leopards and the majestic sun (hello!), and, really, what would life be without avocados? But I think Mother Nature's greatest gift to humanity is the color* GREEN. *Happily, she wasn't stingy with her gift, so we get to enjoy myriad shades of this gorge color— fresh* GRASS, *moss, pine trees, Bells of* IRELAND, *olive trees.*

I think Mother Nature's chef d'oeuvre is the green of April leaves. Just when you're at your wit's end from the brutality of winter, suddenly new shoots spring up—bright chartreuse, green with a jolt of yellow—and you suddenly feel optimistic. When I want to create an uplifting, Happy Chic magical space, I channel Mother Nature and go with APRIL *green.*

Choose chartreuse. For the wallpaper in my powder room, I modernized a classic brocade print by cleaning up the lines and dousing it in a bright, saturated hue. The lighter the green, the fresher it is.

GREEN

IS GROOVY!

SPECS

DOLLS

GO **Green**

✦ *Fill a bowl with bright green limes.* **Why?** *Because I said so, and because limes go with everything.*

✦ *Plonk a chartreuse umbrella stand in your hallway. It says,* **HELLO!**

✦ *Add* ***verdant luxury*** *to a small room with an oversized fig tree.*

✦ *Dress up as a* ***leprechaun*** *next Halloween.*

✦ *Cover a bottle rack in* ***green glass bottles,*** à la *Marcel Duchamp.*

✦ *For a deep sleep, wallpaper your bedroom ceiling with* ***vines and foliage.***

SARASOTA MODERN

ROOMS

Hariri & Hariri**Houses**

ART & TODAY

With its swirly Paul Smith rainbow rug and spring-green banquette, this New York breakfast room is a Happy Chic place to eat your Lucky Charms.

The softer side of green
is on display in fashion designer Nanette Lepore's townhouse parlor. We chose celadon curtains to establish swanky style and pick up the color of her signature peacock feather–patterned rug. (When decorating a room, always pick the rug first and match paints and fabrics to it.)

FOR A FLORAL ELEMENT WITH ARCHITECTURAL PRESENCE, GO FOR BIG BRANCHES— THEY REALLY FILL A SPACE AND BRING HEIGHT TO LOW FURNISHINGS.

Lava glaze gives my Saturn vases a pitted texture, creating a depth of surface that plays off the simple silhouettes. I love how the edge of the glaze goes brown, lending a complementary accent.

The mossy green curtains in my Palm Beach pad have just the right degree of saturation and depth to temper harsh sunlight and offer a reprieve from the elements. This stroke of color forms a dramatic backdrop for a seating vignette with a complementary orange table.

My love/hate pillows were inspired by Robert De Niro's knuckles in *Cape Fear*—how love can turn into hate, and how each exists only when seen in context of its opposite. Hate makes love possible, makes it more real and incredible. The same is true with colors: a deliberate juxtaposition of opposites draws out each shade's oomph.

MIXING GREEN

BENJAMIN MOORE
··········
BABY FERN 2029-20

BENJAMIN MOORE
··········
GRIZZLY BEAR BROWN 2111-20

BENJAMIN MOORE
··········
ECCENTRIC LIME 2027-30

BENJAMIN MOORE
··········
METALLIC SILVER 2132-60

BENJAMIN MOORE
··········
GUACAMOLE 2144-10

BENJAMIN MOORE
··········
BRICK RED 2084-10

WHEN IN DOUBT:
Green + *brown.* The most natural color combo on earth goes together like birds and feathers.

CHIC AND CLASSIQUE:
Green + *gray.* Go for lime green with icy silver. The sophistication of gray makes the boldness of green possible.

TRICKY TREAT:
Green + *red.* Danger—this can go too Christmas! For guidance, think Gucci's pairing of forest green with maroon.

In kitting out Liz Lange's country sunroom, we brought the outdoors in. Though the furniture is swanky—an Arne Jacobsen Swan chair, a nailhead-studded screen, brass cocktail tables—the sofa's peat-colored upholstery echoes the greenery outside and creates the sense that you're relaxing in nature.

GREEN-SPIRATION!

MUSe

Lilly Pulitzer

In life you have a choice. You can either limit your color palette and surround yourself with gray, beige, and taupe, or you can embrace the exuberant kaleidoscopic life-enhancing phantasmagoria of COLOR.

COLOR IS JOY. *Color is the fabulous dinner party you had when you set your table with orange placemats. Color is the unforgettable vacation you spent in Capri. Color is the flaming sunset. Color is nature, color is fun.*

Color is Lilly Pulitzer and Lilly Pulitzer is color.

Lilly somehow captures all the majesty of Mother Nature with a no-holds-barred, sloppy, exuberant, naïve, frolicsome spirit. In Lilly's expert paws, colors can't clash and why would they? Purple, pink, green, turquoise, navy, yellow, orange, all in one freaky print, all garish, all kapow, all meow, all **FUN.**

If you can manage to overlook the fact that Lilly Pulitzer has built a gigantic fashion empire, you get the feeling that Lilly Pulitzer has never worked a day in her life. Lilly has played every day in her life, and the mega-brand that is Lilly Pulitzer is an accidental by-product of a life spent being silly, gamboling in the surf, having the occasional cocktail, and embracing the colorful, gorgeous, sublime majesty of Mother Nature.

PRECIOUS METALS

When Andy Warhol covered
the walls of his Factory with aluminum foil, he and his coconspirators made an important discovery: metallics make magic.

Whether it's **SILVER** leaf, bold **GOLD,** platinum glamour, beaten **COPPER,** shredded Mylar, or antique **BRASS,** metallic surfaces add drama and fantasy to your decor.

I have often found that my decorating clients are metallic-shy. They are scared of seeming flashy or grandiose. "Adding some precious metals to your home is just like adding a little **JEWELRY** to your outfit," I tell them. "And, if it was good enough for Andy Warhol and Marie Antoinette, it's certainly good enough for YOU!"

My client's art-centric Manhattan living room is a well curated mix of objects, from Jennifer Bartlett's painting to the Yves Klein coffee table in unexpected pink. The gold hand and foot chairs by artist Pedro Friedeberg take center stage, injecting a bit of flash that's echoed by the gold-leafed Rococo chairs and my gilded Nelson Lantern lamps.

Shiny accents can look incredibly luxe, as demonstrated by my design for Nanette Lepore's opulent boudoir. A pair of '30s sconces flanking the fireplace infuse the room with Hollywood glamour, while the matte silver leather covering the armchair and ottoman pick up the sheen. Other metallic accents add arresting twinkle: the chrome fire screen, the painting's gold frame, the mirrored coffee table.

BRING IN THE **BLING** WITH MIRRORED FURNITURE—A CLEVER WAY TO REFLECT SURROUNDING COLORS AND PATTERNS.

GOLD IS BOLD. SILVER IS KINKY.

MINI **Muse**:
SPRATLING SILVER

Feeling shy about shiny? Find inspiration in Taxco-based jewelry designer William Spratling, who breathed new life into Mexican silverwork in the '30s and '40s. He created stunning repoussé baubles for the fashion flock that mixed silver and gold together.

I treated this bedroom vignette like an exquisite jewelry box with lots of sparkly baubles, reiterating the sheen of the gilded bed frame with shimmery Bonetti side tables, a turquoise-encrusted box, and my radiant and regal Versailles Etoile vase, glazed with real gold.

PEDAL TO THE **Metal**

- ✦ *Hang **copper jelly molds** on a knotty pine kitchen wall for a '60s-mod vibration.*

- ✦ ***Silver-leaf** the frame of a youthful portrait of your glamorous granny and make her look like a movie star.*

- ✦ ***Rust is delicious.** Leave your metal flea-market finds on the roof for six months and then spray/seal them with Krylon paint.*

- ✦ ***Gold-leaf** your entryway for a flattering effect. (Don't forget to paint the wall red before leafing, to add warmth to the gold.)*

- ✦ *Don't polish your silver too often. It's better with a little **patina.***

- ✦ ***Have an American Gigolo moment:** down with the frumpy drapes, up with the steel Venetian blinds!*

GO FOR THE GOLD!

MIXING METAL

WHEN IN DOUBT:
Gold + *white* eliminates the risk of gaudiness and tones down the flash.

> BENJAMIN MOORE
> ··········
> AUTUMN GOLD
> 2152-30

\+

> BENJAMIN MOORE
> ··········
> WHITE WISP
> OC-54

CHIC AND CLASSIQUE:
Turquoise + *silver*.
Nothing is groovier than a silver-leafed ceiling in an ice-blue room.

> BENJAMIN MOORE
> ··········
> TURQUOISE HAZE
> 2060-60

\+

> BENJAMIN MOORE
> ··········
> GRAY SKY
> 2131-70

TRICKY TREAT:
Silver + *gold*.
Conventional wisdom says to choose one or the other. But who cares about convention? Go for it! Just do it with conviction, balancing the two hues rather than just letting one dominate.

> BENJAMIN MOORE
> ··········
> SILVER HALF DOLLAR
> 2121-40

\+

> BENJAMIN MOORE
> ··········
> STUART GOLD
> HC-10

MU*S*e

Grace Jones

☆ *She was an unapologetic gender bender.*

☆ *She made the accordion cool again.*

☆ *She dyed the inside of her mouth with* PINK *dye.*

☆ *She treated her own body as an art piece.*

☆ *She popularized the Flat Top Fade haircut.*

☆ *She was wildly inspirational to me as a teen growing up in The Middle of Nowhere, New Jersey.*

☆ *She wore giant Issey Miyake hats.*

☆ *She rocked* BODY PAINT.

☆ *She made music that was as creative as her ensembles.*

☆ *She wore costumes that make Lady Gaga look like Laura Bush.*

☆ *She's still at it, more* outré *and* SHINY *than ever.*

People who are afraid of color are afraid of **LiFe.**

Granny Smith apples, key limes, and string beans...These are a few of my favorite **GREENS.**

Fuchsia feels fresh... ➝ in a particular way...

TURQUOISE: Run, don't walk … and then dive right in!

Temper your brights— **tomato red**, aquamarine, *kelly green*— with a dash of **TAUPE.**

Let your color Id run wild.

magenTA= *a tingling sensation* in ALL *your chakras.*

A black patent leather chair says, "I'm fancy, and I read *French Vogue.*"

Tan LeaTHer ADDS BUTCH GLAMOUR. THINK ABOUT IT.

Don't neuter your **NEUTRALS**— *a zippy accent color will ignite your* **BEIGE.**

If you love it like crazy, it will work.

Sometimes **ordinary** can be **extra-ordinary**— paint your walls

PAPER-BAG-BROWN.

➤ *Benjamin Moore Peanut Shell 2162-40*

Only a pansy is scared of

PRIMROSE.

ORANGE & PINK

is far chic-er than you think.

If colors are

FReNEMiES,

invite them to the UN for a peace summit… *avocado* and *orange*, bonjour!

LAVENDER

doesn't have to be Granny— **TeaM iT WiTH TeaL** *and watch it pop.*

Add gravitas with gray felt.

A soupçon of celery will perk you right up.

LEMON YELLOW

is

LIME GREEN's BEST FRIEND.

Schedule a playdate.

QUaKER GRaY

is the new chocolate brown.

Anything goes if you mix colors of the same value.

When in doubt, go tonal—pair

FUCHSIA with *flamingo*, **cerise** with **cinnamon**, *cerulean* with **INDIGO**.

PHOTO CREDITS

INDEX

Aarnio, Eero, 95
Aarons, Slim, 43
Accessories
  in black and white, 52–53
  in blue, 19, 20–21
  in chambeige, 85
  in chartreuse, 111
  in green, 112, 114
  in orange, 103
  in red and pink, 64
  Saturn vases, 117
  in silver and gold, 130–133
Arad, Ron, 71

Baby blue, musings on, 9
Barbie, 62–63
Bartlett, Jennifer, 127
Bathrooms
  chartreuse brocade wallpaper
    in, 110
  glass accessories for, 20
  orange as accent color in, 99
Beene, Geoffrey, 43
Black and white combination,
    42–53
  with brown, 46
  furnishings in, 44–45, 50, 52–53
  incorporating into lifestyle,
    suggestions for, 47
  with silver, 46
  with turquoise, 46
Blue, 8–25. See also Turquoise
  as accent color in dining room,
    104–105
  baby blue, musings on, 9
  incorporating into lifestyle,
    suggestions for, 16
  mixing with other blues, 18
  mixing with other colors, 18

multiple shades of, in seating
    area, 13
  with red and white, 70
  selected items in, 17
  stair risers painted in tones of, 25
Bonetti, Mattia, 95, 132
Brown, colors to combine with
  black and white, 46
  blue, 18
  green, 119
  orange, 92–93, 96
  red, 70
Bunting, Kyle, 95

Capri, Isle of, 40–41
Carlyle Hotel, 47
Castle, Wendell, 24
Chairs. See also Chippendale chairs
  by Arne Jacobsen, 120
  by Eero Aarnio, 95
  by Eero Saarinen, 59
  by Pedro Friedeberg, 126–127
  Rococo style, 50, 126–127
  by Ron Arad, 71
  by Wendell Castle, 24
Chambeige, 74–89
  furnishings in, 81
  incorporating into your lifestyle,
    84
  moods created by, 82, 86–87
  in open-plan living space,
    76–77
Chartreuse
  brocade wallpaper in bathroom,
    110
  furnishings in, 111
Chippendale chairs
  in black, 129
  in chartreuse, 111

in lemony yellow, 32
in orange, 96
Color, formula for using, 6

Draper, Dorothy, 47

Flooring. *See also* Rugs
    white cowhide carpet by Kyle
        Bunting, 94–95
    white painted floor, 104–105
Fornasetti, Barneba, 54
Fornasetti, Piero, 54–55
Friedeberg, Pedro, 127

Gernreich, Rudi, 49
Glass accessories, in blue, 19,
    20–21
Gold
    red combined with, 70
    silver combined with, 135
    with white, 94, 134, 135
    William Spratling accessories,
        130–131
Goldin, Nan, 95
Gray, colors to combine with
    green, 119
    orange, 96
    yellow, 39
Green, 108–121
    with brown, 119
    furnishings in, 113, 114–115
    with gray, 119
    incorporating into lifestyle, 114
    mixing with other colors, 119
    with red, 119
Greenbrier Resort, 47

Halston, 15
Hawa Mahal palace, Jaipur, India,
    106
Hicks, David, 15
Horst, Horst P., 43

India, colors of, 106
Isle of Capri, 40–41

Jacobsen, Arne, 120
Jaipur, India, 106
Jones, Charles Hollis, 95

Jones, Grace, 136–137

Klein, Yves, 127

La Scalinatella Hotel, Isle of Capri,
    40–41
Lange, Liz, country house interiors of
    dining room, 32
    sunroom, 120
Latner, John, 95
Lepore, Nanette, townhouse
        interiors of
    boudoir, 128–129
    parlor, 116–117
Louboutin, Christian, 57
Lowit, Roxanne, 15

Magenta, 61
Metallics, 124–135
    as accent color in boudoir,
        128–129
    incorporating into lifestyle,
        suggestions for, 133
    mixing with other colors, 135
Minter, Marilyn, 66
Moffitt, Peggy, 49
Mollino, Carlo, 54

Natural materials. *See also*
        Chambeige
    colors and textures of, 78–79,
        84
    in open-plan living space, 76–77
Navy blue, orange combined with,
    96
Needlepoint pillows
    in black and white, 49
    in blue hues, 12
    with exuberant designs, 7
    in red, 65
Nelson Lantern lamps, 126–127
Neutral palette. *See* Chambeige
Nicola L., 95

Orange, 90–105
    as accent color, 99, 100
    controversial nature of, 91
    in dining room, 104–105
    furnishings in, 102–103
    mixing with other colors, 96
    musings on, 101

pink combined with, 101,
106–107

Panton, Verner, 49, 91
Parco dei Principi Hotel, Sorrento,
Italy, 26–27
Paschke, Ed, 13
Pink, 57–63
as accent color, 57, 66–67
bold pattern with, in small space,
57
furnishings in, 66–67
orange combined with, 101,
106–107
using in small space, 60
Ponti, Gio, 26–27
Post Ranch Inn, Big Sur, CA, 80
Pucci, Emilio, 31
Pulitzer, Lilly, 122–123

Red, 56–71
brown with, 70
furnishings in, 64, 67
green with, 119
incorporating into your lifestyle,
suggestions for, 70
mixing with other colors, 70
string sculpture in, 67
white and blue with, 70
yellow with, 70
Richardson, Terry, 87
Rococo style
chairs, 50, 126–127
mirror, 71
Rudolph, Paul, 87
Rugs
blue-striped runner, 24
matching paints and fabric to,
116
oriental patchwork, 82
by Paul Smith, 115

Saarinen, Eero
tulip chair, 59
tulip tables, as ping-pong table
base, 68–69
Silver
black and white with, 46
and blue hexagon pattern, in
stairwell, 14–15
green with, 119

turquoise with, 135
William Spratling accessories,
130–131
Slater, Anne, 16
Smith, Paul, 115
Spratling, William, 130–131
Starck, Philippe, 87
Stone, Sly, 13

Tablescaping, 12
Turquoise
as accent color, 10–11, 19
with black and white, 46
painted wall in entry foyer, 23
with yellow, 32

Versailles Etoile vase, 132
Von Teese, Dita, 57
Vreeland, Diana, 72–73, 106

Wallpaper
blue hexagon-patterned, in
stairwell, 14–15
boldly-patterned, in powder
room, 60
chartreuse brocade, in bathroom,
110
covering ping-pong table with,
68–69
Warhol, Andy, 125
White
and black (See Black and white
combination)
with gold, 94, 134, 135
with red and blue, 70

Yellow, 28–39
with black, 39
blue with, 18
with gray, 39
healing properties of, 29
incorporating into lifestyle,
suggestions for, 39
mixing with other colors, 39
red with, 70
selected items in, 34–35
turquoise with, 32

Zeisler, Claire, 68

THE JONATHAN ADLER MANiFESTO

I believe that your home should make you happy.

I believe that when it comes to decorating, the wife is always right. Unless the husband is gay.

I believe in carbohydrates and to hell with the puffy consequences.

I believe minimalism is a bummer.

I believe handcrafted tchotchkes are life-enhancing.

I believe tassels are the earrings of the home.

I believe in the innate chicness of red with brown.

I believe in being underdressed or overdressed, always.

I believe celebrities should pay full price.

I believe in Palm Beach style: Louis chairs, chinoiserie, Lilly Pulitzer, The Breakers circa '72.

I believe my designs are award-winning even though they've never actually won any.

I believe in Aid to Artisans.

I believe dogs should be allowed in stores and restaurants.

I believe you should throw out your BlackBerry and go pick some actual blackberries.

I believe my lamps will make you look younger and thinner.

I believe in irreverent luxury.